The Usborne
Healthy
Cookbook

Fiona Patchett

Designed by Nancy Leschnikoff

Illustrated by Joelle Dreidemy

Recipes by Catherine Atkinson

Photography by Howard Allman

Food preparation by Dagmar Vesely and Abigail Wheatley

Americanization: Carrie Armstrong   U.S. Cooking Consultant: Barbara Tricinella

Contents

What is healthy food?

Having a healthy diet is all about eating the right amount of lots of different foods. This book is packed with mouth-watering recipes to make you feel healthy and full of energy. With each recipe, you can discover more about the ingredients and why they are so good for you.

On pages 4-5, you can find out what makes a good, balanced diet. And on pages 6-7, there are some handy hints on how to get started in the kitchen.

fresh food versus junk food

Making meals and snacks yourself, using fresh food, is much better for you than buying junk food, such as hamburgers, chips or candy. Some ready-made meals that look as though they contain healthy ingredients often have lots of added salt, sugar or fat. They may taste fine, but they don't contain many nutrients - the good things your body needs to be healthy. You can find out more about these on the next few pages.

Cooking food

Cooking makes food easier for your body to digest, but it can also reduce the amount of nutrients. The best way to cook food and keep the nutrients is by steaming, baking, grilling, making soups or stews, and stir-frying instead of deep-frying.

What should you eat?

Different foods contain different nutrients, that do different jobs in your body. You need to eat a variety of foods to make sure you are getting a good range of nutrients. Here are the main ones:

Carbohydrates

Carbohydrates give you energy. There are two forms of carbohydrates: starches and sugars. Starchy foods, such as bread, potatoes, rice and pasta, are better for you than sugary foods.

Natural sugars, in foods such as honey or fruit, contain some nutrients, but sugar you buy in packets and find in cakes, chocolate or sweetened drinks is much less good for you.

Protein

Protein helps you grow and it helps your body repair itself. You can find it in lean meat, fish, cheese, eggs, milk, nuts and beans.

Fat

Your body uses fat to keep you warm, to protect organs like your kidneys, and to help you absorb vitamins. Although it's high in energy, too much of some fats can be dangerous. Avoid fatty foods such as chips and try ones that also contain other nutrients, such as milk, meat or oily fish.

Vitamins and minerals

Different vitamins do different jobs: some fight germs, some help you grow, and others help your body to use the energy you get from food. For essential chemical processes to take place in your body, you need small amounts of almost 40 different vitamins and minerals. If you eat a balanced diet, you should get them all.

Calcium is a mineral, found in foods such as milk and cheese, which makes your bones and teeth strong.

Iron is a mineral which is essential for healthy blood. It is found in meat, fish and vegetables, such as spinach.

Fiber

Fiber is vital for keeping food moving through your body and preventing diseases. It helps make waste soft enough to pass out of your body. Fiber is found in fruit, vegetables, whole-grain bread and pasta, whole-grain cereals, brown rice, beans and nuts.

If you have a sweet tooth, you might like sweet potatoes. As well as tasting sweeter, they contain more nutrients than ordinary potatoes.

Cheese is a good source of calcium, which is good for bones and teeth.

To get enough different vitamins and minerals, you should eat five portions of fruit and vegetables a day.

Nuts and seeds are an excellent source of protein and minerals.

How much should you eat?

Nutritionists divide food into the six groups below. You should eat most from groups 1, 2 and 3 and least from group 6, as shown in the pie chart on the right.

1. Bread, potatoes, rice, pasta and cereals

These are starchy carbohydrates and you should eat lots, for energy. Eat 6 oz. of these every day. At least half should be whole grains.

2 and 3. Fruit and vegetables (fresh, frozen or canned)

Eat at least five servings (2½ cups) of different fruits and vegetables a day, for vitamins, minerals and fiber. Different-colored fruits and vegetables contain different nutrients, so eat as much variety as you can.

4. Meat, fish, eggs, nuts, beans and lentils

Eat 5 oz. of these foods a day. They provide protein, which helps you to grow, so they're especially important when you are young.

5. Milk, cheese, yogurt

Eat two or three servings (2-3 cups) a day. These foods contain calcium, which is good for your bones and teeth - especially important when you're growing.

6. Foods containing fat and/or sugar

Don't eat too many of these. Examples of foods that are mostly fat and sugar include cakes, ice cream and cookies.

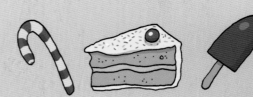

What should you drink?

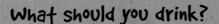

Your body needs liquid to function properly. Try to drink six or seven glasses of water a day - more if it is hot or you are exercising a lot. Pure fruit juice is good for you as it contains vitamins. A glass a day counts as one of your five portions. Fruit 'drinks' do not count, as they are usually high in sugar and artificial chemicals and low in real fruit.

Getting started

Here are some tips to help your cooking go smoothly. Read each recipe before you start to cook, and make sure you've got all the ingredients listed, as well as all the equipment you'll need. Always wash your hands before you start cooking.

Fruit and vegetables

You should wash most fresh fruit and vegetables before you use them. If vegetables have a lot of dirt on them, scrub them clean with a brush that is only used for food. Wash lettuce leaves and herbs, then use a salad spinner to dry them. If you don't have a salad spinner, gently dry them on a clean paper towel.

Measuring

Use measuring spoons and cups to measure liquids and solids. When you add a spoonful of something to a mixture, the ingredient should lie level with the top of the spoon, not heaped up.

Use measuring spoons to measure teaspoons and tablespoons.

Use kitchen scissors to cut up fresh herbs such as parsley or chives.

If you are using basil, you should tear the leaves, not cut them, as this helps to keep the flavor.

Your range

Always cook things in the middle of your oven. If you have a fan oven, you will need to shorten the cooking time or lower the temperature. Look in the oven's instruction book to see what is recommended. Don't open the oven door while you're cooking, unless the recipe tells you to, or you think something might be burning.

To avoid knocking saucepans over, always turn the handles to the side of the cooker. And remember to turn off the stove and burners when you've finished cooking.

Remember to put on oven gloves before you pick up anything hot.

Flavoring your food

Your body doesn't need much salt and too much can be bad for your heart. Most of the recipes in this book don't contain added salt. For more flavor, try adding a pinch of spice, chopped herbs or squeezed lemon juice after you've finished cooking. A 'pinch' is the amount you can pick up between your first finger and thumb.

Making breadcrumbs

1. To make breadcrumbs, use bread that is two or three days old. Cut off the crusts and tear the slices of bread into pieces.

2. Put the bread into a bowl. Mix with a hand-held blender until you get fine crumbs. Be careful of the blender's sharp blades.

If you don't have a blender, you can grate some bread on the big holes of a grater. Slightly stale bread works best.

Food processors and blenders

Food processor   Jug-style blender

Sifting

Hand-held blenders are the easiest to use, but you can use a food processor or a jug-style blender instead.

Put the food in the blender or processor. Put on the lid and twist it firmly. Turn it on to blend the food. Be careful of the sharp blades.

You need to sift some ingredients, such as flour, to get rid of any lumps. Put the flour in a sieve over a bowl and shake the sieve.

Breaking an egg

Beating eggs

Crack an egg sharply on the edge of a bowl. Push your thumbs into the crack and pull the shell apart, so the egg falls into the bowl.

When the eggs are in the bowl, use a fork to stir them quickly and lightly, until the yolks and whites are mixed together.

Ingredients

Serves 4

1 lime
2 tablespoons honey
4 tablespoons orange juice
a few sprigs of fresh mint
1 red apple
1 small pear
2 nectarines
2 oranges
5 oz. fresh raspberries
5 oz. seedless green grapes

Variations

You can make fruit salad with all sorts of combinations of fruit. Here are some ideas:

Tropical fruit salad
Mix pineapple, papaya, bananas and kiwi fruit in pineapple juice.

Orchard fruit salad
Mix apples, pears, plums and blackberries in apple juice.

Healthy food facts

Fruit is a great source of vitamin C, as well as other vitamins, minerals and fiber. Red, orange, yellow, green and purple fruits and vegetables contain different nutrients, so try to eat a 'rainbow' of foods a day to get all the nutrients you need.

fresh fruit salad

1. Cut the lime in half. Squeeze out the juice and pour it into a large bowl. Stir in the honey and orange juice. Wash the mint and dry it on a clean paper towel.

2. Remove the mint leaves from the stems. Use scissors to cut the leaves until you have about a tablespoonful. Add the cut mint leaves to the bowl.

3. Wash the apple, pear and nectarines. Cut the apple and pear into quarters and cut out the cores. Cut the quarters into slices and add them to the bowl.

4. Stir the fruit so it is coated in the liquid. Cut the nectarines in half and take out the pits. Cut each half into slices. Stir the nectarines into the mixture too.

5. Peel the oranges and divide them into segments. Add them to the bowl. Wash the raspberries and grapes. Dry them on a paper towel. Add them to the bowl too, and gently stir everything together.

fruit smoothies

Strawberry smoothie

1. Peel the banana and cut it into thick slices. Rinse the strawberries and dry them on a paper towel. Cut out the stalks. Cut the strawberries in half.

2. Put the fruit in a jug-style blender with the yogurt. Put the lid on firmly and blend the ingredients together until they are smooth. Pour the drink into a glass.

Mango smoothie

1. Slice the mango lengthways, on both sides of the pit. Peel off the skin. Then, cut the flesh away from the pit and put it all in a jug-style blender.

2. Squeeze out the juice from half a lime. Add the lime juice, apple juice and honey to the blender. Put on the lid and blend everything together. Pour it into a glass.

Ingredients

One strawberry smoothie:

1 banana
6 large strawberries
5 oz. carton plain yogurt

One mango smoothie:

1 ripe mango
½ lime
½ cup apple juice
2 tablespoons honey

If you don't have a jug-style blender or smoothie-maker, you can use a hand-held blender instead.

Variations

You could use lots of other combinations of fruits too. For example, try replacing the strawberries with a mixture of raspberries and blueberries.

Raspberry and blueberry smoothie

Strawberry smoothie

Mango smoothie

A fruit smoothie gives you one of your five portions of fruit and vegetables a day.

Ingredients

Serves 6

2 oz. whole hazelnuts
1 tablespoon sunflower oil
3 tablespoons honey
5 oz. rolled oats
1 oz sunflower seeds
1 tablespoon sesame seeds
2 oz. dried apricots
1 oz. raisins

Healthy food facts

Apricots are rich in vitamin A, which is good for your eyesight and helps prevent diseases. They also contain iron for your blood. Dried apricots are even better than fresh ones, as the same nutrients are concentrated into a smaller amount. Just three dried apricots count as one portion of fruit.

Nuts provide vitamin E, which is good for your skin, hair and blood, and helps prevent diseases. They contain protein, which is especially useful if you are vegetarian and do not get protein from meat.

Oats are rich in starchy carbohydrate. They provide you with enough energy to last you through the morning and keep you from wanting to snack. They can help you to concentrate too.

Golden granola

1. Preheat the oven to 350°F. Put the hazelnuts in a clean plastic food bag and close the end. Roll a rolling pin over the nuts to crush them.

2. Put the sunflower oil and honey into a pan. Stir them together with a wooden spoon over low heat until the mixture is warm and runny. Then, turn off the heat.

3. Add the hazelnuts, oats, sunflower seeds and sesame seeds to the pan. Stir everything together until all the ingredients are well coated.

4. Carefully pour the mixture onto a baking tray. Use a spoon to spread it out into an even layer. Bake it in the oven for 15 minutes, until it turns golden.

5. While the granola is baking, cut the apricots into small pieces. When the granola is ready, use oven gloves to take the tray out of the oven.

6. Leave the granola for 5 minutes to cool. Then, pour it into a bowl, breaking it into small clusters with your fingers. Stir in the apricots and raisins.

Serve the granola with low-fat milk or low-fat yogurt. Scatter some fresh chopped fruit over the top.

Variations

You could try these variations to the recipe, or make up your own:

Tropical granola

2 oz. brazil nuts

1 tablespoon sunflower oil

3 tablespoons honey

5 oz. rolled oats

1 oz. sunflower seeds

1 tablespoon dried coconut

2 oz. dried pineapple

1 oz. banana chips

Apple and cinnamon granola

2 oz. whole hazelnuts

1 tablespoon sunflower oil

3 tablespoons honey

½ teaspoon ground cinnamon to add to the honey and oil

5 oz. rolled oats

1 oz. sunflower seeds

1 tablespoon sesame seeds

2 oz. dried apples

1 oz. raisins

Eating breakfast

After a night's sleep, your body and brain need fuel to get going for the day. Eating a breakfast like this granola - that contains whole-grains, fiber and protein - will help your concentration. Include milk or yogurt to give you calcium for your bones and teeth. Add fresh fruit, a fruit smoothie, or a glass of fruit juice to give your body a boost of vitamins and minerals.

Ingredients

Serves 4

1 onion

2 medium-sized potatoes

1 tablespoon olive oil

1 tablespoon water

4 oz. lean ham,
   thickly sliced

¾ cup (4 oz.) peas, fresh or
   frozen (put them on a
   plate to defrost)

1 tablespoon chopped fresh
   parsley

5 medium eggs

⅔ cup low-fat milk

a shallow 8-9 inch
   ovenproof dish

Variations

Try adding green beans,
broad beans or other
vegetables to this omelette.
If you are a vegetarian you
could add feta or cheddar
cheese instead of ham.

Pea and ham omelette

Preheat the oven to 350°F.

1. Cut the onion in half, cut each half into thin slices, then cut the slices into small pieces. Peel the potatoes and cut them in half. Then, cut them into small cubes.

2. Put the oil and water into a frying pan, over low heat. Add the onions and potatoes. Cook them for 10 minutes, stirring occasionally. Turn off the heat.

3. Cut the ham into ½ inch squares. Add the ham, peas and parsley to the pan. Stir everything together. Wipe a little oil around the inside of the ovenproof dish.

4. Spoon the mixture into the dish and spread it into an even layer. Then, break the eggs into a large bowl. Add the milk and beat them together with a fork.

5. Pour the egg mixture over the ham and vegetables. Put the dish into the oven and bake the omelette for 40 minutes, until it is set and golden brown.

6. Push a knife into the middle of the omelette. If runny egg comes out, cook it for 5-10 minutes more. Run a knife around the edge and cut the omelette into wedges.

Most omelettes are cooked in a frying pan, but this one is baked, so it has much less fat. It is packed with nutritious peas, potatoes and ham, so it makes a complete meal in itself.

Hard-boiling eggs

1. To hard-boil an egg for a salad, heat some water in a pan until it is boiling. Put the egg into the pan with a spoon. Gently boil it for 10 minutes. Turn off the heat.

2. Carefully lift the egg out with a spoon. Put it into a bowl of cold water to cool. Tap it gently on the edge of the bowl until the shell cracks. Then, peel off the pieces.

Healthy food facts

Eggs are a great source of protein, vitamins and minerals. The yolk is rich in iron, which helps your blood carry oxygen around your body. Always wash your hands after handling raw eggs, as they can contain harmful bacteria.

Milk contains protein, vitamins and minerals. It is a good source of calcium for your bones and teeth. Choose low-fat milk, which contains less fat.

Peas are full of protein. They are rich in a B vitamin that is good for your heart, nerves and muscles. Frozen peas are just as good for you as fresh ones.

Ingredients

Serves 4

1½ lbs. ripe tomatoes
   (about 10)
1 red onion
1 medium carrot
1 stick of celery
1 medium potato, weighing
   about 6 oz.
1 tablespoon olive oil
1 clove of garlic
½ vegetable bouillon cube
2 tablespoons tomato paste
½ teapsoon dried basil or
   mixed herbs
ground black pepper
4 tablespoons low-fat milk
4 small sprigs of fresh basil

Healthy food facts

Celery is a good source of the mineral potassium, which is good for your kidneys, digestion and nervous system.

Tomatoes contain vitamin C, which fights germs, heals bones and wounds, and helps you absorb iron. The red color in tomatoes, and other red foods, is called lycopene. It helps protect your body from diseases. Cooked tomatoes contain even more lycopene than raw ones because the lycopene is more concentrated.

creamy tomato soup

1. Cut each tomato into quarters. Cut out the green cores and throw them away. Cut the quarters into small pieces. Cut off the ends of the onion, peel it and cut it in half.

2. Slice the onion, then cut it into small pieces. Peel the carrot and cut off the ends. Wash the celery and cut off the ends. Cut the carrot and celery into thin slices.

3. Peel the potato and cut it into 6 chunks. Put the oil into a large saucepan and heat it for 20 seconds. Add the onion and cook it for 3 minutes, stirring it often.

4. Add the celery, carrot and potato to the pan. Peel the garlic and crush it into the pan. Cook the vegetables for 3 more minutes, stirring them every now and then.

5. Put half a bouillon cube in a heatproof container. Pour 2 cups of boiling water into the cup. Add the tomato paste and stir until the bouillon cube has dissolved.

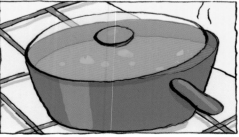

6. Add the stock, tomatoes, herbs and a pinch of pepper to the pan. Bring the soup to a boil. Turn down the heat. Then, put a lid on the pan, leaving a small gap.

7. Let the soup bubble gently for 20 minutes. Turn off the heat and let it cool for 10 minutes. Using a hand-held blender, carefully blend the soup until it is smooth.

8. Add the milk to the soup. Gently heat it until it bubbles. Then, ladle the soup into bowls. Put a sprig of fresh basil in each bowl before you serve it.

Soup is easy to eat even when you are not feeling well. This one is especially good for you as the tomatoes are full of vitamin C.

Variations

You can make as many types of soup as there are vegetables. Most vegetables work well with onions, but there are lots of combinations you could try. Here are some ideas:

* Leek and potato

* Pea and mint

* Mushroom

* Lentil and tomato

* Carrot and coriander

Some vegetables take longer to cook than others. To test whether a vegetable is ready, push a fork into one piece. If it is tender, that means it's cooked.

You can use a blender to make any soup smooth. To make a chunky soup, just cut the vegetables into small pieces and don't blend them.

Thai noodle soup

Ingredients

Serves 4

6 green onions
1 red pepper
4 oz. mangetout or
    sugar snap peas
4 oz. baby sweetcorn
½ vegetable bouillon cube
4 cups hot water
½ lime
2 thin slices fresh root ginger
2 teaspoons sunflower oil
2 tablespoons soy sauce
5 oz. egg noodles
a few sprigs of fresh
    coriander
5 oz. large peeled, cooked
    shrimp or prawns

1. Cut off the ends of the green onions and remove the outer layer. Then, cut the onions into diagonal slices. Cut the ends off the pepper and cut it in half.

2. Remove the seeds from the pepper and cut it into strips. Cut the ends off the mangetout or sugar snap peas and cut them in half lengthways. Cut the corn in half lengthways, then across.

To give this soup extra flavor, squeeze some lime juice over it.

A bowl of Thai noodle soup is a meal in itself. It provides carbohydrate from the noodles, vitamins and fiber from the vegetables and protein from the shrimp or prawns.

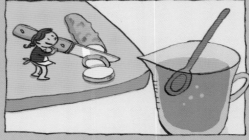

3. Put half a bouillon cube into a heatproof container and pour over half of the hot water. Stir until the bouillon cube has dissolved. Squeeze the juice from half a lime.

4. Cut two slices of ginger. Add the ginger and lime juice to the broth. Stir the broth, then put it aside. Put the oil into a large pan and heat it gently.

5. Add the green onions to the pan and fry them for 1 minute. Pour the broth into the pan. Then, add the soy sauce and the rest of the hot water.

6. Simmer the broth for 3 minutes. Then, using a wooden spoon, remove the ginger and throw it away. Add the noodles and the prepared vegetables to the pan.

7. Turn up the heat and let the soup simmer for 2½ minutes. Wash the coriander and dry it on a clean paper towel. Use scissors to cut the leaves into small pieces.

8. Add the shrimp to the soup. Let it simmer for another 5 minutes. Turn off the heat. Add a tablespoon of coriander leaves, then ladle the soup into bowls.

Healthy food facts

Prawns and shrimp are an excellent source of protein. Unlike many other forms of protein, they are low in unhealthy fat. They do contain a healthy type of fat, omega-3 fatty acids, which are good for your brain, heart, circulation and joints. Prawns and shrimp are full of minerals, including calcium, which is good for your bones and teeth. But they are quite salty, so don't eat *too* many.

Ginger is the root of a tropical plant and is often included in Asian dishes. It has a spicy flavor and gives many health benefits. For centuries, ginger has been used as medicine to help improve circulation and digestion, and prevent travel sickness, coughs and colds.

Variations

Thai noodle soup is also delicious made with tofu instead of shrimp or prawns. Tofu is made from soy beans and provides protein, starchy carbohydrate, fiber and lots of vitamins and minerals. Add about 11 oz. tofu, cut into cubes, to the soup, instead of the shrimp or prawns.

17

Ingredients

Makes 8 rolls

2 cups bread flour

1½ cups whole wheat flour

¾ teaspoon salt

¼ cup (2 oz.) sunflower seeds

1½ teaspoons rapid-rise yeast

1 teaspoon dried mixed herbs
(optional)

1⅓ cups low-fat milk, plus
a little extra

3 teaspoons honey

2 tablespoons sunflower oil

sunflower seeds, poppy seeds
and sesame seeds to
sprinkle on top

Healthy food facts

Whole wheat flour
contains the most nutritious
parts of the wheat grain,
which are taken out of
white flour. It is a starchy
carbohydrate and contains
fiber, minerals and vitamin E,
which is good for your eyes,
skin and liver.

Seeds, such as sesame seeds,
poppy seeds, sunflower seeds
and pumpkin seeds, are high
in calcium, which is good for
your bones and teeth.

Honey and seed bread

1. Use a sieve to sift the flour into
a large bowl. Pour any bran left
in the sieve into the bowl too. Stir
in the salt, sunflower seeds, yeast
and herbs, if you are using them.

2. Put the milk, honey and oil in
a pan and heat them very gently
until they are just warm. Make a
hollow in the middle of the flour,
then pour in the milky mixture.

3. Stir everything together with
a wooden spoon, to make a soft
dough. Sprinkle some flour over
a clean work surface and put the
dough onto it.

4. Then you need to massage,
or knead, the dough. Press the
heels of both hands into it. Push
it away from you firmly. Fold the
dough in half and turn it around.

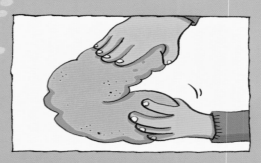

5. Continue pushing the dough
away from you, folding it over
and turning it around for 10
minutes, until it feels smooth
and springy.

6. Use a paper towel to wipe
a little cooking oil around
the inside of a bowl. Put the
dough in the bowl and cover
it with foodwrap.

7. Leave the dough in a warm place for an hour, until it has risen to twice its original size. Knead it again for a minute to squeeze out any air bubbles.

8. Use a paper towel to wipe oil over a baking tray. Break the dough into 8 pieces. Roll them into balls, flatten them slightly and put them on the tray.

9. Preheat the oven to 425°F. Wipe oil onto some foodwrap. Put it over the rolls, oiled side down. Leave them in a warm place for 30 minutes to rise.

10. Take the foodwrap off the rolls. Brush each roll with some milk, then sprinkle on some seeds. Bake the rolls in the oven for 12-15 minutes.

11. Take the rolls out of the oven and leave them on the baking tray for a few minutes. Then, lift them onto a wire rack to cool.

This homemade bread doesn't contain the added sugar and preservatives that may be found in store-bought bread, and it has less salt too.

open sandwiches

Ingredients

Serves 4

4 slices of dark rye bread for each recipe

Prawn salad

1 tablespoon low-fat crème fraîche

1 teaspoon tomato purée

2 teaspoons lime juice

4 oz. shrimp

4 cherry tomatoes

5 or 6 lettuce leaves

Egg mayonnaise

2 eggs

1 tablespoon low-fat mayonnaise

2 teaspoons lemon juice

alfalfa sprouts or cress

Crab and avocado

1 tablespoon low-fat mayonnaise

2 teaspoons red pesto

7 oz. can white crab meat

1 avocado

Tuna and sweetcorn

1 tablespoon low-fat mayonnaise

7 oz. can tuna

4 oz. can sweetcorn

5 or 6 lettuce leaves

Apple, cheese and celery

1 apple

1 stick of celery

1 teaspoon lemon juice

1 tablespoon low-fat mayonnaise

3 oz. grated cheese

Prawn salad

1. Put the crème fraîche, tomato purée and lime juice in a bowl and mix them together. Stir in the shrimp. Cut the tomatoes in half on a chopping board.

2. Wash and dry the lettuce leaves, then tear them into bite-sized pieces. Arrange the tomatoes, lettuce and prawn mixture on each slice of bread.

Egg mayonnaise

1. Hard-boil the eggs and peel them (see page 13). Put the eggs on a chopping board and carefully slice them with a knife. Then, cut the slices into little squares.

2. Put the mayonnaise and lemon juice in a bowl and mix them. Stir in the eggs. Put the mixture onto the bread. Wash and dry the alfalfa sprouts or cress and add them.

crab and avocado

1. Mix together the mayonnaise and pesto in a bowl. Open the can of crab meat. Tip it into a sieve to drain it. Add it to the bowl and mix it in. Cut the avocado in half.

2. Remove the avocado stone. Slice the flesh lengthways. Use your thumbs to push the slices out of the skin. Spread the crab onto the bread. Arrange the avocado on top.

Tuna and sweetcorn

1. Open the cans of tuna and sweetcorn. Use a sieve to drain off the liquid from both. Put them in a bowl with the mayonnaise. Mix everything together.

2. Wash and dry the lettuce leaves, then tear them into bite-sized pieces. Arrange the lettuce on the bread. Then, spoon on the tuna and sweetcorn mixture.

Apple, Cheese & Celery

1. Cut the apple into quarters. Peel them, then cut out the cores. Grate each quarter of apple on the big holes of a grater. Put the apple in a bowl. Stir in the lemon juice.

2. Wash the celery stick and cut it into thin slices. Add the celery, grated cheese and mayonnaise to the apple. Stir everything together. Spoon the mixture onto the bread.

Open sandwiches are a good way of eating a variety of toppings without filling up on much bread.

Shrimp, lettuce and lemon

Smoked salmon and hard-boiled egg

Slices of cheese and tomato

Healthy food facts

Rye is a type of grain used to make bread and crisp breads. It is rich in vitamins, minerals and fiber, and makes a good alternative to wholewheat bread. Rye bread and pumpernickel bread are often used for open sandwiches because they are firm enough to hold lots of toppings.

More variations

Bacon, arugula and tomato
Mix low-fat mayonnaise and a little Dijon mustard, then spread it onto the bread. Grill some lean bacon and put it onto the bread, with the arugula and slices of tomato.

Smoked salmon and ricotta
Spread a layer of ricotta cheese on the bread, then lay on a thin layer of smoked salmon. Squeeze on a little lemon juice and snip some chives or dill on top.

You can use any of these fillings to make normal sandwiches for a packed lunch or picnic, using two slices of bread for each sandwich. It's best to use softer bread than rye bread for this, though.

Ingredients

Serves 4-6

Tomato and basil

2 tablespoons olive oil

2 teaspoons balsamic vinegar

ground black pepper

8 large fresh basil leaves, plus a few small sprigs to garnish

8 ripe tomatoes

1 loaf ciabatta bread

1 large clove of garlic

Smoked mackerel pâté

2 smoked mackerel fillets, weighing 6 oz

½ lemon

3 oz low-fat cream cheese

a few sprigs of fresh dill

ground black pepper

1 loaf whole-grain bread

Save any leftover pâté or tomato in an airtight container in the refrigerator. It will keep for about 3 days.

Healthy food facts

Mackerel is a type of oily fish, like sardines, salmon or fresh tuna. Oily fish is rich in protein, vitamins and minerals. It is the best source of omega-3 fatty acids, a healthy type of fat (see page 17 to find out more).

Try to eat a portion of oily fish once or twice a week.

Toast toppings

Tomato and basil

1. Put the olive oil, vinegar and a pinch of ground black pepper in a bowl. Whisk them together with a fork. Tear the basil into small pieces and add them too.

2. Cut the tomatoes into quarters. Carefully cut out the core at the top of each one and throw it away. Cut the tomatoes into small squares and stir them into the mixture.

3. Using a serrated knife, carefully cut slices off the ciabatta loaf, each about ½ inch thick. Cut as many slices as you want to serve.

4. Put the slices into a toaster. Put the toaster on a fairly low setting and toast the bread until it is golden. If it needs to toast for a little longer, put it in again.

5. Cut the clove of garlic in half. Rub the cut side of the garlic over one side of each slice of toast.

6. Spoon the tomato mixture over the toast. Garnish each piece of toast with a sprig of basil.

These toppings make a healthy
snack or a light meal.

Smoked mackerel pâté

1. Use your fingers to peel off
the skin of the mackerel fillets.
Remove any small bones. Put the
fillets into a bowl. Then, squeeze
the juice from half a lemon.

2. Add the lemon juice to the
bowl. Use a fork to mash the
mackerel. Add the cream cheese,
then keep on mashing until
everything is mixed together.

3. Stir in a pinch of black pepper.
Slice and toast the bread (see steps
3 and 4 opposite). Spread on the
pâté and decorate each one with
a piece of dill.

Ingredients

Serves 4

2 heads of baby lettuce or
   mixed greens
½ cucumber
2 sticks celery
5 ripe tomatoes

For the herby dressing:

1 tablespoon mixed fresh
   herbs
3 tablespoons olive oil
1 tablespoon white wine
   vinegar
½ teaspoon Dijon mustard

a jar with a lid

Healthy food facts

Olive oil is made from the juice of crushed olives. Olive oil and sunflower oil are both unsaturated fats. These are much better for your heart than the saturated fats found in butter and red meat.

Super salads

1. Cut off the bottom of each lettuce and remove the leaves. Wash all the leaves and dry them. Tear the larger leaves into smaller pieces.

2. Cut the ends off the cucumber. Then, cut it in half lengthways. Lay each half with the flat side facing down. Cut both halves into thin slices.

3. Wash the celery sticks and cut them into slices. Cut the tomatoes into quarters. Carefully cut out the green core at the top of each piece and throw it away.

4. Put the lettuce leaves, celery, cucumber and tomatoes into a large bowl. For the dressing, wash the herbs and dry them on a clean paper towel.

5. Use scissors to cut up the herbs. Put them in a clean jar with the olive oil, vinegar and mustard. Screw on the lid very tightly. Just before you serve the salad, shake the jar well to mix the dressing. Then, drizzle it over the salad and mix it in.

This Niçoise salad is made from a delicious mix of cooked and raw ingredients, providing a wide range of vitamins.

Cool Combinations

For variety, add different ingredients to the basic salad.

Apple and walnut salad

Cut 2 red apples into quarters and cut out the cores. Slice the apples thinly. Stir the slices into the dressing. Then, add them to the salad with some chopped walnuts.

Bacon and avocado salad

Halve 2 ripe avocados and remove the pits. Cut the flesh into cubes and push it out of the skin. Stir the avocado into the dressing. Grill some lean bacon, then cut it into squares. Add it to the salad with the avocado.

Niçoise salad

Use a fork to break up some drained, canned tuna. Add the tuna, some cooked green beans, half a can of anchovies, 12 pitted black olives and 2 hard-boiled eggs, cut into quarters.

Oriental salad

Add bean sprouts and cooked shrimp. Scatter sesame seeds on top. Make the dressing using 1 tablespoon of sesame seed oil and 2 tablespoons of sunflower oil, instead of the olive oil. Add a tablespoon of soy sauce and a teaspoon of honey, but leave out the herbs.

Ingredients

Serves 4

Guacamole

2 ripe avocados
½ lemon
1 clove of garlic
2 drops pepper sauce
4 ripe tomatoes
3 tablespoons sour cream

Hummus

14 oz. can chickpeas
½ lemon
1 large clove of garlic
½ teaspoon ground cumin
2 tablespoons olive oil
½ cup low-fat sour cream
ground black pepper

Vegetable sticks to dip in

1 carrot
1 red pepper
2 celery sticks
½ cucumber

You can also try dipping in raw baby sweetcorn, button mushrooms, broccoli, cauliflower, or toasted pitta bread, cut into strips.

Delicious dips

Guacamole

1. Cut each avocado in half lengthways and remove the pit. Cut the flesh into cubes, then use your thumbs to push them out of the skin into a bowl.

2. Squeeze ½ a lemon and add the juice to the bowl. Crush the garlic into the bowl. Add 2 drops of pepper sauce. Use a fork to mash the avocado until it is smooth.

3. Cut the tomatoes into quarters. Scoop out the seeds with a teaspoon. Then, cut out the green core at the top of each piece. Cut the tomatoes into small pieces.

4. Add the tomatoes and sour cream to the bowl and stir them in. Serve it right away, or squeeze a little lemon juice over the top to stop it from going brown.

Hummus

1. Put the chickpeas into a sieve and rinse them under cold water. Drain them and pour them into a large bowl. Squeeze ½ a lemon and add the juice to the bowl.

2. Crush the garlic into the bowl. Add the cumin, olive oil, sour cream and a pinch of black pepper. Use a hand-held blender to blend the mixture until it is smooth.

Vegetable sticks

1. Wash all the vegetables and cut the ends off them. Peel the carrot. Cut the pepper in half and remove the seeds.

2. Cut all the vegetables into strips of about 3 inches long. It is easier to cut long vegetables in half first, before you cut them lengthways.

Serve the hummus and guacamole with a mixture of vegetable sticks and strips of toasted pitta bread.

Healthy food facts

Avocados are a good source of vitamin E, which is good for your skin, hair and blood, and helps to prevent diseases. They also contain unsaturated fat, which is better for your heart than saturated fat.

Garlic is good for your blood and circulation, and may help to prevent coughs and colds. It is rich in potassium, which is good for your kidneys, digestion and nervous system.

Ingredients

Serves 4

½ lime
a little sunflower oil
2 tablespoons honey
½ teaspoon dried oregano
a pinch of ground cinnamon
½ teaspoon ground paprika
4 skinless, boneless chicken
   breasts
1 medium carrot
6 green onions
1 small red pepper
1 small yellow pepper
8 soft flour tortillas

Healthy food facts

Chicken is low in fat, but high in protein, which helps you to grow. It is rich in B vitamins, which give you energy during the day and help you sleep at night. It also contains the mineral zinc, which is good for your skin and digestion, and helps to heal wounds.

After you have handled raw chicken, wash your hands thoroughly, as well as the board, plates and utensils you've used. Chicken can contain harmful bacteria until it has been cooked.

Chicken fajita wraps

1. Squeeze the juice from half a lime. Put it in a large bowl, with a teaspoon of sunflower oil, the honey, oregano, cinnamon and paprika. Whisk it all together.

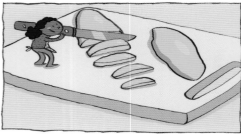

2. Wash the chicken and put it on a chopping board. Cut off any bits of white fat and throw them away. Cut each breast across into 8 strips. Add them to the bowl and stir them in.

Use a different board to chop the vegetables.

3. Wash your hands thoroughly. Cut the ends off the carrot and peel it. Cut the ends and outer layers off the green onions. Cut each onion lengthways into strips.

4. Cut the ends off both peppers. Cut them in half and remove the seeds. Cut the peppers and carrots into strips about 3 inches long. Preheat the oven to 400°F.

5. Put 1 tablespoon of sunflower oil into a large frying pan and heat it over medium heat for 1 minute. Carefully add the chicken to the pan with a spoon.

6. Cook the chicken for 5 minutes, stirring it with a wooden spoon, until the color has changed all over. Use a slotted spoon to take it out of the pan and onto a clean plate.

The word fajita (pronounced fa-hee-ta) describes any food served in a soft flour tortilla. This type of food originated around the border between Mexico and Texas, and is sometimes called Tex-Mex food. You can serve it with guacamole and low-fat sour cream.

Stir the vegetables all the time.

7. Put the strips of carrot into the pan and cook them for 2 minutes. Then, add the green onions and peppers and cook them for 2 minutes.

8. Put the tortillas onto a baking tray and put them in the oven. Put the chicken back in the pan. Cook everything for 3-4 minutes. Then, take the tortillas out of the oven.

9. Put some chicken and vegetables on top of each tortilla, leaving the bottom half and sides empty. Fold the bottom half over the filling. Fold over one side, then the other.

29

Ingredients

Baked sweet potatoes

1 large sweet potato per
    person

Baked sweet potatoes are
delicious filled with any of
the sandwich toppings from
pages 20-21. Or try adding
guacamole or hummus
(pages 26-27), tzatsiki (pages
34-35), baked beans, low-fat
cottage cheese or salad.

Potato wedges

Serves 4

3 large potatoes
1 tablespoon olive oil
mixed herbs

Healthy food facts

Potato skins contain fiber
and the mineral potassium,
so it is much better for you
to eat the skins as well as the
inside of a potato.

Sweet potatoes, unlike
ordinary potatoes, count
toward your five portions of
fruit and vegetables a day.
They contain vitamin A,
which is good for your
eyesight and helps your
body fight off disease. All
potatoes provide starchy
carbohydrates, but the
carbohydrates in sweet
potatoes will give you
energy for longer.

Potatoes

 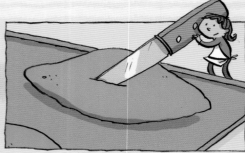

1. Preheat your oven to 350°F.
Scrub the potatoes with a brush
to remove any dirt. Prick the skins
with a fork, then put them on a
baking tray.

2. Bake them in the oven for an
hour. Gently push a knife into one
potato. If it is soft inside, it is ready.
If it is hard, put the potatoes back
in the oven for 5 more minutes.

3. While the potatoes are cooking, prepare the filling you want. Then,
take the potatoes out of the oven. Carefully cut a large cross in the top
of each one and open them out. Use a fork to mash the insides a little to
soften them. Then, spoon in your filling.

1. Preheat the oven to 400°F. Scrub
the potatoes clean. Cut them in
half, then into chunky wedges.
Spoon the oil and herbs onto a
baking tray and add the wedges.

2. Turn the potatoes with two
spoons, so they are lightly covered
in oil. Cook them in the oven for
45 minutes, lifting them out and
turning them every 15 minutes.

Roasted vegetables

1. Preheat your oven to 400°F. Cut the top off the onion and peel it. Cut it in half, then cut each half into three wedges, from top to bottom.

2. Cut the ends off the zucchini, eggplant and peppers. Cut the eggplant in half lengthways. Cut each half into 1 inch chunks. Cut the zucchini into 1 inch slices.

3. Cut both peppers in half and remove the seeds. Cut them into wide strips. Put all the vegetables into a large roasting pan with the olive oil and rosemary.

4. Crush the garlic into the pan. Stir everything together so it is well coated with oil. Put the pan in the oven for 30 minutes, or until the vegtetables are tender.

Roasting vegetables brings out all their flavor and sweetness. It is an easy way to cook a variety of vegetables together, without using too much oil.

Ingredients

Serves 4

1 red onion
3 zucchini
1 eggplant
1 red pepper
1 yellow pepper
3 tablespoons olive oil
3 sprigs of fresh rosemary
1 clove of garlic

Variations

You can roast almost any combination of vegetables in the same way. Try roasting carrots, squash, new potatoes, parsnips and onions together.

Healthy food facts

Onions contain calcium and vitamin C, which helps to prevent coughs and colds, heals bones and wounds, and helps your body to absorb iron.

Peppers are rich in vitamins A and C. The red color in red peppers is lycopene, which helps to protect your body from diseases.

Eggplant and **zucchini** are rich in vitamin C, as well as potassium, which is good for your kidneys, digestion and nervous system.

Ingredients

Serves 4

12 oz. red and yellow
  cherry tomatoes
a little olive oil
1 clove of garlic
12 oz. dried pasta shapes
7 oz. can tuna fish
½ lemon
a handful of arugula leaves
2 oz. grated Parmesan
  (optional)

Variations

Here are more toppings to try:

* Gorgonzola cheese,
  spinach and pine nuts

* Sardines, tomatoes and
  black olives

* Roasted vegetables
  (see page 31)

* Tomato sauce
  (see pages 36-37)

Healthy food facts

Tuna from a can doesn't
contain as many nutrients as
fresh tuna, but it is still rich
in protein and B vitamins,
and it is easy to prepare.
Use canned tuna in oil or
springwater, but not in
brine, which is very salty.

Tuna pasta

1. Preheat the oven to 400°F.
Cut the tomatoes in half on a
chopping board. Put them into
a roasting pan. Then, crush the
garlic into the pan.

2. Add half a tablespoon of
olive oil to the pan. Gently stir
the tomatoes so they are coated
in the oil. Put the pan into the
oven for 15 minutes.

3. Half-fill a large pan with
water. Add a tablespoon of olive
oil. Heat the water until it is
boiling. Then, put the pasta in
the pan and stir it.

4. Heat the water until it is
boiling again. Then, turn down
the heat, so that it is bubbling
gently. Cook the pasta for as
long as it says on the package.

5. To see if the pasta is cooked, lift
out a piece with a spoon, rinse it
under cold water and bite it. It
should be tender, but not soggy.
If it isn't ready, cook it for longer.

6. Turn off the heat. Then, pour the
cooked pasta into a colander and
drain it, by gently shaking it over
the sink. Pour the pasta back into
the pan and add the tomatoes.

Pasta is the perfect way of adding starchy carbohydrates to a meal to fill you up.

7. Open the can of tuna. Pour it into a sieve and drain off the oil. Use a fork to break it into large chunks. Add it to the pasta. Squeeze the juice from half a lemon.

8. Add the tuna and lemon juice to the pasta. Stir them in for a few seconds. Wash and dry the arugula leaves, then stir them in. Serve the pasta. Add Parmesan if you like.

Healthy food facts

Pasta is made from flour and eggs. It is a starchy carbohydrate, so it will fill you up and give you lots of energy. For more fiber, try using whole-wheat pasta.

There are many shapes and sizes of pasta. Thin pasta, such as capellini or spaghetti, works well with light sauces.

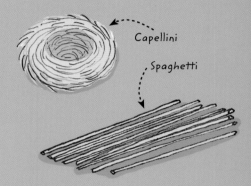

Capellini

Spaghetti

Thicker shapes, such as fusilli, penne or conchiglie, work well with chunkier sauces.

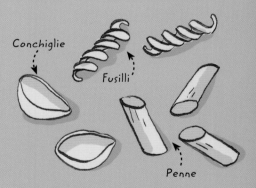

Conchiglie

Fusilli

Penne

Try adding tiny pasta shapes, such as rotini or stellete, to soups or casseroles to make them more filling.

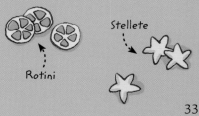

Stellete

Rotini

Ingredients

Makes 16 falafels

1 slice bread
1 egg
14 oz. can chickpeas
a little olive oil
1 large clove of garlic
1 tablespoon lemon juice
1 medium carrot
½ teaspoon ground coriander
1 teaspoon ground cumin
a pinch of ground turmeric
2 tablespoons fresh parsley

For the tzatsiki:

½ cucumber
1 tablespoon fresh mint
¾ cup strained plain low-fat yogurt*

4 pieces whole-grain pitta
   bread
some lettuce leaves

* To strain the yogurt, place it in a coffee filter, inside a mesh strainer, over a bowl. Let the liquid drain off overnight.

Healthy food facts

Chickpeas are extremely nutritious. As well as being an excellent source of protein, they contain iron for your blood and calcium for your bones. They are also a good source of fiber, which helps you to digest your food. Try adding chickpeas to soups, casseroles and curries.

Herby falafels

Preheat the oven to 400°F. Cut a piece of baking parchment the same size as a baking tray and lay it on the tray.

1. Put the bread in a large bowl. Use a hand-held blender to make it into breadcrumbs. Break the egg into a small bowl. Beat it with a fork. Stir it into the breadcrumbs.

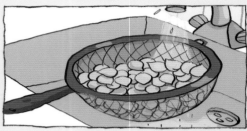

2. Put the chickpeas into a sieve and rinse them under cold water. Drain them and pour them into the bowl with the breadcrumbs. Add 1 teaspoon of olive oil.

3. Use the blender to make the mixture into a paste. Peel and crush the garlic and add it to the bowl. Add 1 tablespoon of juice squeezed from half a lemon.

4. Peel the carrot and cut off the ends. Hold it firmly and grate it on the big holes of a grater. Add it to the bowl, with the ground coriander, cumin and turmeric.

5. Use scissors to cut up the parsley or coriander into small pieces. Stir them into the other ingredients. Pick up a heaped teaspoonful of the mixture and roll it into a ball.

6. Put the ball on the baking tray and flatten it slightly. Put more balls of mixture on the tray, leaving spaces between them. Brush each one with a little oil.

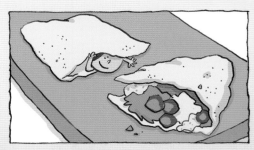

7. Bake the falafels in the oven for 15 minutes until they are crisp. Meanwhile, make the tzatsiki. Cut the cucumber in half lengthways and scoop out the seeds.

8. Cut the cucumber into tiny squares. Use scissors to cut the mint leaves into small pieces. Then, mix the mint, cucumber and yogurt together in a bowl.

9. Heat the pitta bread in the oven for 2 minutes. Cut each piece into 2 pockets. Spread some tzatsiki inside each half, then fill them with lettuce and falafels.

Falafels are usually deep-fried, but these are baked in the oven, which uses a lot less fat.

Ingredients

Makes 4

For the crust:

1 cup bread flour
⅓ cup whole wheat flour
1 teaspoon rapid-rise yeast
¼ teaspoon salt
¼ cup low-fat milk
2 teaspoons olive oil

For the tomato sauce:

2 cloves of garlic
1 teaspoon olive oil
14 oz. can chopped tomatoes
½ teaspoon dried oregano or
    mixed herbs
1 teaspoon tomato paste
ground black pepper

For the toppings:

1 cup (5 oz.) ready-grated
    mozzarella cheese
A combination of:
sliced button mushrooms
ham cut into squares
pitted black olives
canned pineapple
canned anchovies
canned tuna
bottled artichoke hearts
crumbled feta cheese
arugula leaves
sliced tomatoes

Mini pizzas

1. Sift both flours into a big bowl.
Pour in any bran left in the sieve.
Stir in the yeast and salt and make
a hollow in the middle. Gently
warm the milk and oil in a pan.

2. Pour the milky mixture into the
hollow. Use a wooden spoon to mix
everything together to make a
dough. Sprinkle flour over a clean
work surface. Put the dough onto it.

3. Follow steps 4-6 on page 18
to knead the dough. Leave the
dough in the bowl, in a warm
place for an hour, until it has
risen to twice its original size.

4. To make the sauce, peel and
crush the garlic. Put it in a pan
with the oil. Add the tomatoes,
herbs, tomato paste and a pinch of
black pepper to the pan.

5. Heat the sauce over medium
heat for 15 minutes, stirring it
with a wooden spoon. Then, take
the pan off the heat and leave
the sauce to cool.

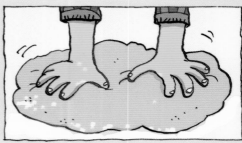

6. Lift the dough out of the bowl
and put it onto a floury surface.
Knead it for one minute. Heat your
oven to 425°F. Wipe a little oil over
a baking tray.

7. Divide the dough into 4 pieces. Sprinkle some flour onto a rolling pin. Put one piece of dough on the work surface. Roll out the dough until it is about 6 inches across.

8. Lift the dough onto the tray. Roll out the other pieces of dough and put them on the tray, too. Spread the sauce onto each pizza crust, leaving a border around the edge.

9. Sprinkle cheese over the top. Then add as many toppings as you like. Bake the pizzas in the oven for 15 minutes until they are crisp and the cheese is golden brown.

These thin and crispy pizza crusts provide you with carbohydrates, but not too much, and the whole wheat flour gives you extra fiber. Pile them high, with as many toppings as you like, to get a good variety of protein, vitamins and minerals.

Ingredients

Serves 4

1 inch piece fresh root
    ginger
1 small orange
1 tablespoon soy sauce
1 tablespoon honey
1 tablespoon white wine
    vinegar
a little sesame oil
3 skinless, boneless chicken
    breasts
8 oz broccoli
1 red pepper
4 oz baby sweetcorn
6 green onions
1 tablespoon sunflower oil
2½ oz cashew nuts

Healthy food facts

Broccoli is rich in vitamin K, which makes your bones stronger and helps to stop bleeding. Like other green fruits and vegetables, such as cabbage, spinach and kiwi fruits, broccoli contains folic acid, which helps your body to function and fight disease.

Cashew nuts are packed with minerals: iron for your blood, magnesium for your bones and heart, phosphorus for your bones and teeth, and zinc for your skin, digestion and to heal wounds.

chicken stir-fry

1. Cut the brown skin off the ginger and throw it away. Cut the ginger into thin slices and cut the slices into thin sticks. Then, cut the sticks into tiny pieces.

2. Squeeze the juice from the orange. Put it in a large bowl with the ginger, soy sauce, honey, vinegar and 1 teaspoon of sesame oil. Whisk everything together with a fork.

3. Wash the chicken breasts. Put them on a chopping board. Cut off any bits of white fat and throw them away. Cut each breast across into strips. Add them to the bowl.

Use a different board to cut the vegetables.

4. Wash your hands. Cut the stem off the broccoli and throw it away. Cut off the florets, then cut them into small pieces. Cut the ends off the pepper, then cut it in half.

5. Remove the seeds from the pepper and cut it into strips. Cut the sweetcorn in half lengthways. Cut the ends and outer layers off the green onions.

6. Cut the green onions across diagonally to make small slices. Heat 1 tablespoon of sesame oil in a large frying pan or wok for 1 minute over a medium heat.

7. Use a slotted spoon to lift the chicken out of the bowl and into the pan. Cook it for 2-3 minutes, stirring it all the time, until the color has changed all over.

8. Take the chicken out of the pan with a clean slotted spoon. Put it on a plate and set it aside. Add the sunflower oil to the pan and heat it for about 20 seconds.

9. Add the broccoli, sweetcorn and pepper. Cook them for 2 minutes, stirring all the time. Add the green onions and cook them for 1 minute. Put the chicken back in the pan.

10. Add the orange mixture to the pan. Stir everything together. Cook it for 5 minutes over high heat until the vegetables are tender. Add the cashew nuts and stir them in.

The stir-fry can be served with egg noodles or rice.

Stir-frying is a good method of cooking, as it uses very little oil. The food is cooked quickly, so it keeps most of its nutrients.

Ingredients

Serves 4

1 inch piece fresh root ginger
1 onion
2 tablespoons sunflower oil
1 clove of garlic
1 teaspoon ground cumin
1 teaspoon ground coriander
½ teaspoon ground turmeric
½ vegetable bouillon cube
½ cup (3 oz.) red lentils
1 small cauliflower
1 medium sweet potato
1 cup low-fat coconut
  milk
1 tablespoon lemon juice
1 cup long-grain rice
fresh coriander to garnish

Healthy food facts

Red lentils are low in fat and high in protein. They are rich in vitamins and minerals, and even count toward your five portions of fruit and vegetables a day. The fiber in lentils reduces cholesterol, a type of fat in your body that may be bad for you when you are older.

Cauliflower is a good source of folate, which protects your body from diseases.

cauliflower curry

1. Cut the brown skin off the ginger and throw it away. Cut the ginger into thin slices and cut the slices into thin sticks. Then, cut the sticks into tiny pieces.

2. Peel the onion and cut it in half. Slice it, then chop it into small pieces. Put the onion in a large saucepan with 1 tablespoon of oil. Heat it for 3 minutes.

3. Crush the garlic into the pan. Add the ginger, ground cumin, coriander and turmeric. Cook them for 1 minute, stirring with a wooden spoon.

4. Put half a bouillon cube into a heatproof container. Add 1½ cups boiling water and stir it until the bouillon cube has completely dissolved.

5. Add the lentils and broth to the pan and bring them to a boil. Put on the lid, leaving a small gap. Lower the heat and let everything cook for 10 minutes.

6. In the meantime, pull any leaves off the cauliflower and throw them away. Cut across the stalk about ½ inch from a floret. Pull the floret out, then cut off another one.

7. Peel the sweet potato and cut it in half, then into ¾ inch cubes. Put a tablespoon of oil into a large frying pan. Add the cauliflower and sweet potato to the pan.

8. Fry the cauliflower and potato on high heat for 5 minutes until they start to brown, stirring them all the time. Add them to the lentils. Add the coconut milk too.

9. Put the lid on the pan, leaving a small gap. Turn down the heat and cook the mixture for 15 minutes. Stir in the lemon juice. Scatter the coriander leaves on top.

Boiling rice

1. Put the rice into a sieve and rinse it under cold running water. This cleans the rice and helps to keep it from getting sticky when it is cooked.

2. Half-fill a pan with water and heat it until it boils. Add the rice and bring it back to boil. Turn down the heat and cook the rice for the time it says on the package.

3. To see if the rice is cooked, take out a few grains with a fork. Let them cool for a few seconds, then eat them. The rice should be firm, but not crunchy.

4. If the rice isn't ready, cook it for longer. Turn off the heat, then pour the cooked rice into a large sieve and drain it by shaking it over the sink.

Dhal (pronounced darl) is the name for this type of thick, spicy lentil curry. It is one of the basic dishes in India.

Ingredients

Serves 4

a little olive oil
8 oz. spinach leaves
4 salmon fillets, each
　　about 5 oz.
1 teaspoon balsamic vinegar
2 teaspoons soy sauce
1 clove of garlic
6 green onions
6 oz. cherry tomatoes

Variations

You can try cooking different types of fish in a packet. Add different combinations of vegetables, such as sliced leeks, carrots or peppers.

Healthy food facts

Salmon is a type of oily fish which contains omega-3 fatty acids, which are good for your brain, heart, circulation and joints. It is also a good source of calcium, which is good for your bones and teeth.

Spinach is high in fiber, vitamins and minerals. It contains vitamin A, which is good for your eyesight and helps to prevent diseases, and the mineral potassium, which is good for your kidneys, digestion and nervous system.

Salmon in a packet

1. Preheat the oven to 400°F. Cut 4 pieces of kitchen foil, each 12 inches square. Brush them with olive oil, stopping a little way from the edges.

2. Wash the spinach leaves in cold water. Let them drain in a colander. Then dry them with a clean paper towel. Divide them between the 4 foil squares.

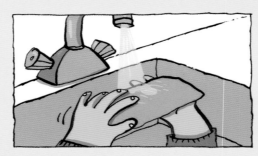

3. Rinse the salmon under cold running water. If you feel any bones sticking out, pull them out and throw them away. Shake the salmon dry.

4. Put one fillet on top of each pile of spinach. Put a tablespoon of olive oil in a bowl with the vinegar and soy sauce. Peel the garlic and crush it into the bowl.

5. Whisk the ingredients in the bowl together with a fork. Cut the ends off the green onions and remove the outer layers. Cut the onions lengthways into strips.

6. Cut the tomatoes in half. Put the tomatoes and slices of green onion into the bowl and mix everything together. Then, spoon the mixture onto the fish.

 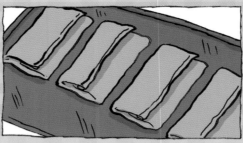 

7. To make the packets, fold the top and bottom edges of each foil square over the fillet. Then, pull the sides together. Fold the side edges over twice to seal the packet.

8. Put the packets onto a baking tray and bake them in the oven for 15-20 minutes. Then, lift them out and let them cool on the baking tray for 5 minutes.

9. Open the foil packets very carefully, watching out for the hot steam inside. Use a spatula to lift the fish and vegetables onto individual plates.

Baking fish in a foil packet is a simple and healthy way to cook, as no nutrients are lost.

Ingredients

Serves 4

1 large onion
1½ lbs lean chuck or arm
    roast, cut into cubes
1 clove of garlic
⅓ cup (2 oz.) barley
1 bay leaf
½ teaspoon dried mixed herbs
ground black pepper
1 tablespoon tomato paste
½ beef bouillon cube
4 large carrots
2 celery sticks

Try adding other vegetables to the casserole, such as chopped red peppers or kidney beans.

Healthy food facts

Beef is a type of red meat. All red meats are high in protein. Beef contains the mineral iron, which is good for your blood. But red meat is high in unhealthy saturated fat, so always use lean meat and cut off the fat. It's best to limit quantities of red meat.

Barley is a type of cereal that is often used to thicken soups and casseroles. Pot barley has more fiber than pearl barley. It also contains the minerals zinc, and phosphorus, which is good for your bones and teeth.

Barley beef stew

1. Preheat your oven to 325°F. * Cut the ends off the onion and peel it. Cut it in half, then cut each half into thin slices. Cut any white fat off the beef.

2. Put the beef and onion into a large ovenproof casserole dish. Crush the garlic into the dish. Add the barley, bay leaf, herbs and a pinch of ground black pepper.

3. Put the tomato paste and half a bouillon cube into a heatproof container. Add 2 cups of boiling water and stir it until the cube has dissolved. Pour it over the beef.

4. Stir all the ingredients in the dish and put on the lid. Put the dish in the oven and cook for 1 hour. Peel the carrots, cut off the ends, then cut them into slices.

5. Wash the celery and cut it into slices. After an hour, carefully take the casserole out of the oven, wearing oven gloves. Add the carrots and celery to the dish.

6. Put the lid back on and put the casserole back in the oven. Cook it for a further 1½ hours, until the meat is tender. Carefully take it out to stir it now and then.

* You can also make this recipe in a slow cooker. Just cook on a medium heat for 8 hours, adding the carrots and celery after 6 hours.

Cabbage & mustard mash

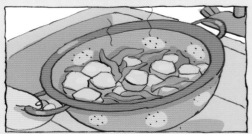

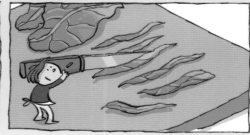

1. Peel the potatoes. Cut them in half, then cut them into large chunks. Put them in a saucepan and cover them with cold water. Heat the water until it boils.

2. Reduce the heat so the water is boiling gently. Put on the lid, leaving a small gap. Cook the potatoes for 12 minutes. Cut the cabbage into slices and wash them.

3. Add the cabbage to the pan and cook it with the potatoes for 4 more minutes. Carefully drain them both through a colander, then tip them back into the pan.

4. Add the margarine, milk, mustard and a pinch of black pepper. Mash the mixture until it is smooth and creamy. Stir it for a minute with a wooden spoon.

Ingredients

Serves 4

1½ lbs potatoes
6 oz. Savoy cabbage
2 tablespoons sunflower
  margarine
3 tablespoons low-fat milk
1 tablespoon wholegrain mustard
ground black pepper

Healthy food facts

Cabbage is rich in fiber, vitamin C and the mineral iron, which is found in the dark green part of the leaves.

Ingredients

Serves 4

1 medium lemon
6 slices whole wheat bread
2 tablespoons sesame seeds
4 teaspoons dried mixed
  herbs
6 tablespoons all-purpose
  flour
ground black pepper
2 eggs
a little sunflower oil
1 lb. cod fillets,
  skinned

For the tomato sauce:

1 small red onion
1 clove of garlic
14 oz. can chopped
  tomatoes
2 tablespoons fresh parsley

Healthy food facts

Cod is very low in fat and packed with protein, vitamins and minerals. It is rich in the mineral iodine, which is good for your brain and helps you grow. It also contains the mineral sulfur, which is good for your hair, skin and nails.

Parsley, like other herbs, adds flavor and is healthy too. Parsley is a good source of the minerals iron, calcium and potassium.

crispy fish fingers

1. For the sauce, peel the onion and cut it in half. Slice it, then chop it into small pieces. Peel and crush the garlic. Put the garlic, onion and tomatoes into a pan.

2. Heat the mixture until it boils, then turn down the heat. Let it simmer for 15-20 minutes, stirring it occasionally. For the fish fingers, finely grate the rind of the lemon.

3. Put the bread in a large bowl. Carefully use a hand-held blender to make it into breadcrumbs. Stir in the rind, seeds and herbs. Pour the mixture onto a large plate.

4. Put the flour onto another plate. Mix in a pinch of ground black pepper. Break the eggs into a shallow bowl. Carefully whisk them with a fork.

5. Preheat the oven to 400°F. Use a paper towel to wipe oil onto a baking tray. Using kitchen scissors, cut the cod across into strips about ¾ inch wide.

6. Take one strip of fish and dip it into the flour, coating it on both sides. Then, coat it in egg, then in the breadcrumb mixture. Put it onto the baking tray.

 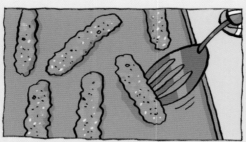 

7. Coat all the strips of fish in flour, then egg, then breadcrumbs and put them onto the tray, spacing them apart. Bake them in the oven for 5 minutes.

8. Take the fish fingers out of the oven. Using a spatula, carefully turn over each one. Put them back in the oven for 5 minutes until they are crisp and golden.

9. Cut the fresh parsley into small pieces and add it to the sauce. Use a hand-held blender to blend the sauce. Then, pour it into a dish to serve with the fish fingers.

Whole-wheat breadcrumbs and sesame seeds provide fiber, vitamins and minerals, as well as giving the fish fingers a crispy texture.

Ingredients

Serves 4

1 lemon
2 leeks
8 oz. button mushrooms
1 tablespoon sunflower
  margarine
1 tablespoon olive oil
1 clove of garlic
½ vegetable bouillon cube
1 cup (8 oz.) quinoa*
1 bay leaf
a pinch of dried thyme or
  mixed herbs
ground black pepper
2 oz. flaked almonds
a few sprigs of fresh parsley

Healthy food facts

Leeks contain vitamin C and they are good for your blood and circulation. They are similar to onions and garlic, but taste sweeter.

Mushrooms are rich in B vitamins and the mineral potassium, which is good for your digestion, kidneys and nervous system.

Leek & mushroom quinoa

1. Grate the rind of the lemon on the small holes of a grater. You will need about a teaspoonful of rind. Then, cut the lemon in half and squeeze out the juice.

2. Cut the roots and dark green leaves off the leeks. Cut the leeks in half lengthways. Rinse each half under cold water to remove any mud or dirt inside.

3. Lay the leeks on a chopping board and slice across them. Wash the mushrooms and dry them on a paper towel. Then cut them into thick slices.

4. Heat the margarine and olive oil gently in a large saucepan for 20 seconds. Add the leeks and mushrooms. Cook them for 5 minutes, stirring them often.

5. Crush the garlic into the pan and cook everything for a few more seconds. Put half a bouillon cube into a heatproof container. Pour in 2 ½ cups of boiling water.

6. Stir the broth until the cube has dissolved. Add the quinoa and broth to the pan. Add the bay leaf, herbs, lemon rind, lemon juice and a pinch of black pepper.

* Quinoa can be found in health food stores and some grocery stores. If you do not find it, you can substitute brown rice for this recipe.

Different Cereals

Quinoa (pronounced keen-wah) is a type of cereal, along with oats, rice, barley, millet, wheat and rye. They all provide starchy carbohydrates to give you energy.

Quinoa grows in South America. It is very low in fat, but is packed with protein, which makes it a great food for vegetarians, who do not get protein from meat. It contains the minerals iron, zinc and even more calcium than milk. It is also rich in folic acid, which helps your body to function properly.

Quinoa is an excellent alternative to pasta or couscous, which are usually made from wheat. Unlike wheat, rye, barley and oats, quinoa does not contain gluten, which is difficult for some people to digest.

Millet is another cereal which is high in starchy carbohydrates and does not contain gluten. It is rich in iron and magnesium.

7. Bring the mixture to a boil. Turn down the heat and cover the pan with a lid. Simmer it gently for 18-20 minutes, or until the liquid has been absorbed.

8. While the quinoa is cooking, toast the almonds (see steps 1 and 2 on page 58). Use kitchen scissors to cut the parsley into small pieces.

9. When all the water has been absorbed, remove the bay leaf and throw it away. Serve the quinoa into bowls, then scatter over the parsley and toasted almonds.

Ingredients

Serves 4

1 clove of garlic

1 inch piece fresh root
   ginger

1 large orange

1 tablespoon honey

1 tablespoon olive oil

3 large lamb steaks, each
   about 6 oz.

1 red onion

1 yellow pepper

1 red pepper

2 zucchini

8 metal or wooden kebab
   sticks. (Soak wooden sticks
   in water first to keep them
   from burning on the grill.)

Healthy food facts

Lamb is a good source of the minerals iron and zinc. Like other red meats, lamb can be high in unhealthy saturated fat, so use lean meat and cut off the fat. Try to eat red meat only once or twice a week.

Couscous is a starchy carbohydrate made from wheat. It is low in fat and high in fiber.

Watercress is packed with vitamins. It is also a rich source of the minerals iron, potassium and calcium.

Lamb kebabs

1. Peel the garlic and crush it into a large bowl. Cut the skin off the ginger. Use a grater to grate its flesh onto a plate. Use your fingers to squeeze its juices into the bowl.

2. Squeeze the juice from the orange and add it to the bowl. Then, add the honey and olive oil to the bowl, too. Whisk the ingredients together with a fork.

Throw away the bone and fat.

3. With a sharp knife, cut out any bone and trim the fat off the lamb. Throw them away. Cut the lamb into ¾ inch cubes. Stir them into the orange mixture.

4. Cover the bowl with plastic foodwrap. Put it in the refrigerator for at least an hour, so that the meat soaks in the juices. Prepare the vegetables.

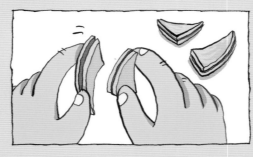

5. Cut the ends off the onion and peel it. Cut the onion in half, then in half again. Cut each quarter in half. Separate each chunk into double slices.

6. Cut the ends off both peppers, halve them and remove the seeds. Cut them into ¾ inch squares. Cut the ends off the zucchini and cut them into thick slices.

7. Push pieces of vegetables and lamb onto each kebab stick, being careful of the pointed ends. Mix up the vegetables and lamb and divide them equally between the sticks.

8. Heat the grill to a medium heat for 5 minutes. Brush the tops of the kebabs with the orange mixture. Then, put them on the grill for 10 minutes.

9. After 10 minutes, carefully turn them over and spoon the rest of the orange mixture over them. Grill them for another 5-10 minutes, until the meat is brown.

You could serve the lamb kebabs with couscous. Stir in some chopped watercress for extra vitamins and minerals.

Ingredients

Serves 4

1 small onion
1 medium carrot
a little olive oil
1 clove of garlic
2 slices whole wheat bread
14 oz. can cannellini beans
14 oz. can red kidney beans
1 tablespoon tomato paste
1 teaspoon dried mixed herbs
½ cup (2 oz.) grated Cheddar
  cheese

Healthy food facts

Beans are a good source of protein and fiber. Kidney beans contain iron, which is good for your blood.

Cheese is also a good source of protein. And it contains the mineral calcium, which is good for your bones and teeth. Cheese can be high in unhealthy saturated fat, so only eat a little each day.

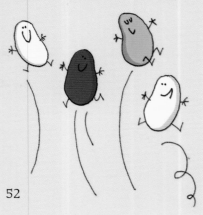

Bean burgers

1. Peel the onion and cut it in half. Cut each half into slices, then cut the slices into small pieces. Cut the ends off the carrot and peel it. Then, use a grater to grate it.

2. Heat 1 tablespoon of oil in a frying pan. Add the onion and cook it for 5 minutes, stirring it often. Add the grated carrot and crush the garlic into the pan.

3. Cook the carrot and onion for 2-3 minutes until they are soft. Turn off the heat. Put the bread in a bowl. Use a hand-held blender to make it into breadcrumbs.

4. Pour the cannellini beans and kidney beans into a colander over the sink. Hold the colander under cold running water and gently shake the beans.

5. Pour the beans into another bowl. Add the tomato paste and herbs. Use the hand-held blender to make the mixture fairly smooth. Then, add the breadcrumbs.

6. Add the carrot mixture and grated cheese to the bowl and mix everything together. Wipe some cooking oil over a baking tray with a paper towel.

7. Heat the broiler or grill to a medium heat. Divide the bean mixture into 8 lumps. Make each lump a circle of about 4 inches across and 1 inch thick.

8. Put the burgers onto the baking tray. Brush both sides of each burger with a little olive oil. Then, put them on the grill or broiler for 5 minutes.

9. Carefully, take the burgers off the grill. Use a spatula to turn them over. Grill them for 5 minutes on the other side until they are turning brown.

These bean burgers are perfect as part of a vegetarian diet, as they are packed with protein. Serve them with homemade tomato sauce (see pages 46-47).

Ingredients

Serves 4

2 leeks
a little olive oil
½ vegetable bouillon cube
2 cups (14 oz.) short-grain
   brown rice
1 cup (5 oz.) frozen peas
2 zucchini
2 oz. sun-dried tomatoes
a few sprigs of fresh parsley
   or mint
½ lemon
1 clove of garlic
9 oz. cooked, peeled shrimps
   or prawns
⅓ cup (2 oz.) grated Parmesan

This recipe uses short-grain
brown rice, but if you use
a different type of rice,
check the package for the
cooking times.

Healthy food facts

Brown rice and white
rice are both good sources
of starchy carbohydrate, but
brown rice will give you
energy for longer. It's also
better for you. Brown rice
contains more fiber than
white rice, as well as
protein, vitamins and the
mineral magnesium, for a
healthy heart and bones.

Brown rice risotto

1. Cut the roots and dark green leaves off the leeks. Cut them in half lengthways. Rinse each half under cold water to remove any dirt or mud inside.

2. Slice the leeks across. Then, put 1 tablespoon of olive oil in a large pan and heat it. Add the leeks and cook them for 5 minutes, stirring them all the time.

3. Put half a bouillon cube in a heatproof container. Pour in 3 cups boiling water and stir until the cube has dissolved. Put the rice in the pan. Stir it to coat it with oil.

4. Pour the broth into the pan. Cover the pan with a lid and let the rice cook on medium heat for 30 minutes. Take the lid off and stir the rice occcasionally.

5. While the rice is cooking, put the peas on a plate to defrost. Cut the ends off the zucchini, then cut them in half lengthways. Cut each half into small cubes.

6. Cut the sun-dried tomatoes into small pieces. Use clean scissors to cut the parsley or mint into small pieces. Then, squeeze the juice from half a lemon.

7. When the rice has been cooking for 30 minutes, heat 1 tablespoon of olive oil in a frying pan. Crush in the garlic. Add the zucchini and peas. Leave the rice on the heat.

8. Cook the vegetables on medium heat for 5 minutes, stirring them all the time. Then, add them to the rice, with the shrimp or prawns, and sun-dried tomatoes.

9. Stir everything together and cook it for 5 more minutes. Take the pan off the heat, then stir in the lemon juice, grated Parmesan and the parsley or mint.

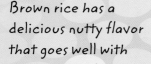

Brown rice has a delicious nutty flavor that goes well with most vegetables.

Variations

As you get used to cooking this risotto, you can experiment by adding your own choice of ingredients. Here are some combinations you could try:

* Carrot, celery and red onion, with a pinch each of ground turmeric and ground coriander

* Asparagus, leeks, peas and fresh parsley

* Mushroom, onion and thyme

* Tomatoes, sun-dried tomatoes, red onion and fresh basil

* Dried cranberries, currants and pine nuts, with a pinch of cinnamon and a little orange juice

Brown rice salad

To make a brown rice salad, first make the risotto and leave it to cool. Add fresh chopped tomatoes, cucumber, celery and green onions. Make the herby dressing on page 24 and drizzle it over the rice.

Ingredients

Serves 4

For the crumble topping:

¼ cup whole wheat flour
¼ cup all-purpose flour
4 tablespoons butter
½ cup ground almonds
¼ cup soft brown sugar
⅔ cup rolled oats

For the fruit filling:

14 oz can peach slices
    in fruit juice
2 cups (8 oz.) frozen or fresh
    raspberries

Healthy food facts

Almonds, like other nuts, are a good source of protein, vitamins and minerals. Almonds are also especially rich in calcium, which is important for your bones and teeth, and magnesium, for your bones and heart.

Peaches are a good source of vitamin A and vitamin C. They also contain the mineral potassium, for your kidneys, digestion and nervous system, and the mineral phosphorus for your bones and teeth.

Peachy crumble

1. Preheat the oven to 375°F. Sift both flours into a large bowl. Pour any pieces of bran left in the sieve into the bowl too. Cut the butter into small cubes.

2. Add the butter to the bowl and stir it in. Use your fingertips to rub it into the flour, until the mixture looks like fine breadcrumbs. Stir in the ground almonds, sugar and oatmeal.

3. Open the can of peaches. Pour them into a sieve over a bowl to catch the juice. Then, arrange the peaches and raspberries in the bottom of an ovenproof dish.

4. Spoon 4 tablespoons of the peach juice over the fruit. Then, use a spoon to scatter the crumble topping over the fruit. Spread the crumble out evenly.

5. Put the crumble into the oven for 30 minutes to cook, until the top is lightly browned. Wearing oven gloves, lift it out of the oven and let it cool for 5 minutes. You can serve it with low-fat frozen yogurt if you like.

Variations

The ground almonds in this crumble topping replace the extra butter and flour that you would find in a traditional crumble. They taste delicious and are far healthier. This topping also includes oatmeal and whole wheat flour, which are also packed with nutrients.

You can make crumble with all sort of different fruit fillings. Here are a few ideas:

* Rhubarb
* Blackberry and apple
* Apricot
* Strawberry and apple
* Plum
* Apple, raisin and cinnamon

Fresh, canned or frozen?

Canned and frozen fruits and vegetables have just as many vitamins as fresh ones, and will count toward your five portions of fruit and vegetables a day. But always check the label to make sure they don't contain added sugar, salt or additives.

Healthy desserts

Some desserts can be good for you, if you choose ones that don't contain too much sugar or saturated fat. Include healthy ingredients, such as fruit, oatmeal, nuts, honey and yogurt. Even a little chocolate isn't bad for you as a special treat.

Ingredients

Serves 4

2 oz flaked almonds

1 cup (5 oz) fresh raspberries

1 cup (5 oz) fresh blueberries

1½ cups low-fat vanilla
  yogurt

4 tablespoons clear, runny
  honey

4 small sprigs of fresh mint to
  decorate

4 glass tumblers or large
  wine glasses

Healthy food facts

Raspberries are an excellent source of fiber, which helps you to digest your food. They are rich in vitamin A and vitamin C, as well as the mineral iron, which is good for your blood. All berries, including strawberries, blueberries and blackberries, are a good source of antioxidants, which are important for helping your body to fight diseases.

Blueberries are a great source of vitamin A, which is good for your eyesight and your brain. They have more antioxidants than other berries and more than most other fruits and vegetables.

Honey berry swirl

1. Spread out the flaked almonds on a baking tray. Put them in the broiler on a medium heat, for 3 minutes. Watch them to make sure they don't burn.

2. When the almonds are golden, carefully take them out of the broiler, wearing oven gloves. Leave the almonds on the tray to cool. Set aside 4 raspberries.

3. Mix together the blueberries and raspberries, then divide half of them between the 4 glasses. Scatter half of the almonds over the berries.

4. Put the yogurt in a mixing bowl. Add 4 tablespoons of honey to the bowl. Swirl the yogurt and honey together once or twice to create a marble effect.

5. Spoon half of the yogurt mixture into the 4 glasses. Scatter the rest of the berries over the yogurt. Scatter the rest of the almonds on top.

6. Divide the rest of the yogurt mixture between the glasses. Put one raspberry and a sprig of fresh mint on top of each glass for decoration.

Healthy food facts

Yogurt is made by adding bacteria to milk, which makes it ferment and thicken. Like milk, yogurt is full of vitamins and minerals. Most yogurt is 'live'. This means the 'friendly' bacteria used to make it are still alive in the yogurt. They help you to digest your food.

Yogurt, milk, butter and cheese are all dairy foods, which are the best source of calcium. If you get enough calcium when you're young, you are less likely to get bone diseases when you are older.

Honey is made by bees gathering nectar from thousands of flowers. It is a great alternative to sugar because it is completely natural. It's also sweeter than sugar, so you don't need as much. Honey contains small amounts of lots of different vitamins and minerals, such as iron, zinc and potassium, as well as antioxidants.

Ingredients

Serves 4

2 oz. dried fruit, such as
  raisins, chopped apricots
  or cherries
1 tablespoon apple or
  orange juice
2 tablespoons dark maple
  syrup
¼ teaspoon ground cinnamon
4 large, crisp, eating apples

Healthy food facts

Apples are an excellent source of vitamins. Cooked apples contain even more vitamin C than raw apples, but they do lose other nutrients, so try to eat both.

Maple syrup comes from the trunk of the maple tree. It is better for you than sugar, because it's natural and contains B vitamins and the minerals, phosphorus, iron and magnesium.

Baked apples

1. Preheat your oven to 375°F. For the filling, put the dried fruit in a bowl with the apple or orange juice, maple syrup and cinnamon, and leave it to soak.

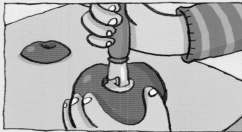

2. Cut a thin slice from the base of each apple. Carefully press an apple corer down through the middle of each apple. Remove the core and throw it away.

3. Use scissors to cut 4 squares of foil, each about 12 x 12 inches. Stand each apple in the middle of a foil square. Spoon in the filling, packing it down tightly.

4. Pull up the foil around the apples and squeeze it on top to make packets. Put the apple packets into an ovenproof dish and bake them in the oven for 30 minutes.

5. Leave the apples in the dish to cool for 5 minutes. Then, carefully open up the foil, lift out the apples and put them into bowls. Serve them with a dollop of low-fat frozen yogurt.

Chocolate bananas

Baking fruit brings out its sweetness and makes a change from fresh fruit. It still has lots of vitamins and counts toward your five portions of fruit and vegetables a day.

1. Preheat your oven to 375°F. Use some kitchen scissors to cut out 4 rectangles of kitchen foil. Each rectangle should measure about 12 x 8 inches.

2. Put a banana in the middle of each foil rectangle. Cut a slit along most of the length of each banana, and about three quarters of the way down into the banana.

3. Break up the chocolate and push a few pieces into each slit. Pull up the foil around each banana and squeeze it to make packets. Put all the packets onto a baking tray.

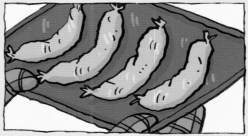

4. Bake the bananas in the oven for 15 minutes. Then, take them out and leave them on the tray to cool for 5 minutes. Take off the foil, then lift the bananas into bowls.

Ingredients

Serves 4

4 large firm bananas
3 oz chocolate

Healthy food facts

Bananas are a good source of carbohydrate. They are easy to digest and are a great way to get a quick boost of energy after exercise. They contain vitamins and minerals, including potassium. They also contain tryptophan, which is good for your brain and can help make you more cheerful.

Chocolate is made with cocoa powder, which comes from the beans of the cacao tree. It contains some healthy minerals, such as iron, which is good for your blood.

Chocolate does contain a lot of sugar and saturated fat, though, so only eat a little as a treat. Chocolate with a cocoa content of at least 70% has a stronger flavor and contains more iron.

Ingredients

Makes 12

1 large carrot
2 eggs
6 tablespoons sunflower oil
1 cup brown sugar
½ cup self-rising flour
⅓ cup whole-wheat flour
½ teaspoon baking powder
1 teaspoon ground cinnamon
1 teaspoon ground ginger

For the icing:

3 oz. light cream cheese
1 teaspoon vanilla
1 cup powdered sugar
⅓ cup (2 oz.) dried apricots,
    dried tropical fruit or nuts

a 12-hole shallow muffin tray
paper baking cups

Healthy food facts

Carrots are an excellent source of vitamins A and C. Other orange and yellow fruits and vegetables, such as carrots, mangoes, apricots, yellow peppers and corn are also high in these vitamins.

Low-fat cream cheese is low in unhealthy saturated fat compared with many types of cheese. It is also rich in calcium and protein.

carrot cupcakes

1. Preheat the oven to 375°F. Put a baking cup into each hole in the muffin tray. Peel the carrot and cut off the ends. Carefully grate it onto a plate.

2. Break the eggs into a small bowl and beat them with a fork. Put the sunflower oil and sugar into a larger bowl and beat them for a minute with a wooden spoon.

3. Add the beaten eggs to the sugar and oil a little at a time. Beat the mixture well after each addition. Then, add the grated carrot and stir it in.

4. Use a sieve to sift both flours, the baking powder, cinnamon and ginger over the mixture. Pour any pieces of bran left in the sieve into the bowl.

5. Gently fold everything together with a metal spoon. Use a teaspoon to divide the mixture between the baking cups. Bake the cupcakes in the oven for 15 minutes.

6. When the cupcakes are firm, take them out of the oven. After a few minutes, lift them onto a wire rack to cool. For the icing, put the cream cheese into a bowl.

Although these are called carrot cupcakes, you can't really taste the carrot.

7. Add the vanilla and mix it into the ricotta with a wooden spoon. Sift the powdered sugar over the mixture. Beat it all together until the mixture is smooth.

8. Spoon the icing onto the cupcakes and spread it out evenly. Cut up some dried apricots, dried tropical fruits or nuts and scatter them on top.

Index

Edited by Sue Meredith and Jane Chisholm; Art Director: Mary Cartwright; Digital imaging: Nick Wakeford; Cover designed by Michelle Lawrence.
With thanks to Anna Gould, Alison McLaughlin and Professor Simon Langley-Evans, Chair of Nutrition, University of Nottingham.
Every effort has been made to trace the copyright holders of material in this book. If any rights have been omitted, the publishers offer
to rectify this in any subsequent editions following notification. The publishers are grateful to the following for their permission to
reproduce material: p.33 © Heinze Winfried/Stockfood Ltd.; p.41 © Uwe Bendar/Stockfood Ltd.